EXPLORE ANCIENT GREECE!

Carmella Van Vleet

Illustrated by Alex Kim

Nomad Press

A division of Nomad Communications

10 9 8 7 6 5 4 3 2 1

Illustrations by Alex Kim

Questions regarding the ordering of this book should be addressed to

Independent Publishers Group

814 N. Franklin St.

Chicago, IL 60610

www.ipgbook.com

Nomad Press

2456 Christian St.

White River Junction, VT 05001

"This logo identifies paper that meets the standards
of the Forest Stewardship Council. FSC is widely
regarded as the best practice in forest management,
ensuring the highest protections for forests and
indigenous peoples."

For Marian and Lyle Van Vleet,
who have always treated me like a daughter.

Other titles from Nomad Press

green press
press
INITIATIVE

Nomad Press is committed to preserving ancient forests and natural resources. We elected to print this title on 30% post consumer recycled paper, processed chlorine free. As a result, for this printing, we have saved:

7 Trees (40' tall and 6-8" diameter)
2,531 Gallons of Wastewater
5 million BTU's of Total Energy
325 Pounds of Solid Waste
610 Pounds of Greenhouse Gases

Nomad Press made this paper choice because our printer, Thomson-Shore, Inc., is a member of Green Press Initiative, a nonprofit program dedicated to supporting authors, publishers, and suppliers in their efforts to reduce their use of fiber obtained from endangered forests.

For more information, visit www.greenpressinitiative.org

Environmental impact estimates were made using the Environmental Defense Paper Calculator. For more information visit: www.papercalculator.org.

CONTENTS

Where in the world was
ANCIENT GREECE?

Have you and your family or friends ever taken a group vote? Have you ever watched the Olympics? Or looked up in the night sky at the constellation Orion? Maybe you've heard about the Trojan Horse, Achilles' heel, or the lost city of Atlantis. Or maybe you've heard of people having a jury of their peers. Guess what! All of these things came from ancient Greece.

Where was ancient Greece? And what was it like to live there? What influence did it have on our world today? In this book, you'll explore ancient Greece, an amazing civilization that reached its height of glory during the years 800–31 BCE. The book will answer many of your questions and share some really cool facts. You'll get to learn about

BCE / CE

As you read, you will notice the letters BCE after some dates. This stands for Before Common Era. The beginning of the Common Era is marked by the birth of Jesus and begins with the year 1. Time before the first year of the Common Era is called as Before Common Era. The years BCE may seem backward, because as time passes, the years actually become smaller in number. A child born in 300 BCE, for instance, would celebrate his or her tenth birthday in the year 290 BCE. Think of it as a countdown to the Common Era.

things like the city of Athens, Mount Olympus, Helen of Troy, and the Spartans. You'll read about the birth of science, mathematics, astronomy, democracy, and even the Olympic games! Along the way, you'll get to do plenty of fun projects and experiments, play games and hear some goofy jokes. Are you ready? Then let's explore ancient Greece!

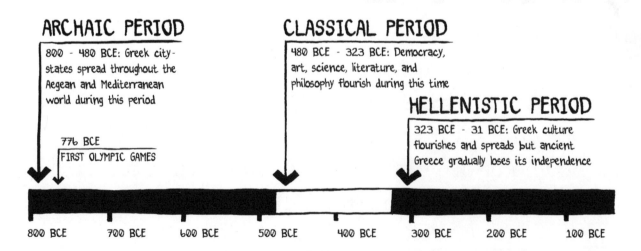

ARCHAIC PERIOD
800 - 480 BCE: Greek city-states spread throughout the Aegean and Mediterranean world during this period

776 BCE
FIRST OLYMPIC GAMES

CLASSICAL PERIOD
480 BCE - 323 BCE: Democracy, art, science, literature, and philosophy flourish during this time

HELLENISTIC PERIOD
323 BCE - 31 BCE: Greek culture flourishes and spreads but ancient Greece gradually loses its independence

800 BCE 700 BCE 600 BCE 500 BCE 400 BCE 300 BCE 200 BCE 100 BCE

WHERE IN THE WORLD WAS ANCIENT GREECE?

ANCIENT GREECE

Today, Greece is a country in the southern part of Europe. The land of ancient Greece included modern-day Greece as well as hundreds of islands in the Aegean, Mediterranean, Adriatic, and Black Seas. Parts of modern-day Turkey, Italy, Egypt, and Spain were also part of the ancient Greek civilization. Ancient Greece wasn't just one country or area. It was a collection of lands. You might be surprised to hear that the people of ancient Greece didn't call themselves Greek. They called themselves Hellenes. And they called their land Hellas. The words *Greece* and *Greeks* came from the ancient Romans.

The land of ancient Greece had lots of mountains. The coastline was jagged. It also had large **plains** where farmers grew crops and people built houses. Winters could be very cold and snowy in the mountains, but most of the rest of ancient Greece was hot and dry.

PLAINS: large, flat land areas.

CITY-STATE: an independent village or town in ancient Greece.

CITY-STATES

Ancient Greece was made up of many **city-states**. A city-state was made up of a central city and surrounding towns and countryside. It's a little like how we have cities surrounded by suburbs.

They were independent, meaning that each of them had their own government and way of doing things. They even had their own kind of money. The Greeks called these city-states "**poleis**." (A "polis" was one city.) People from the countryside and small towns went to the central city to buy things, visit friends, and conduct business. Each polis had an **acropolis**. An acropolis was a high area or hill where people went if there was a battle. The acropolis gave the Greek people a safe place to gather and to watch for the enemy.

ATHENS

Athens was the biggest and most powerful city-state in ancient Greece. It was a bustling place with beautiful buildings and temples. It also had rich farmland and a big harbor, so it was a good place for trading. It was a place of great learning and culture. Some of the ancient world's greatest thinkers, scientists, and artists went to live there. It was *the* place to be! And it was where **democracy** was born. Experts believe that around 500,000 people lived in and around Athens.

Athens' acropolis is one of the most famous in the world. It was there that the Athenians built the Parthenon.

WORDS to KNOW

POLEIS: Greek city-states. Just one is called polis.

ACROPOLIS: a high area or hill where people went during a battle. Also the name of Athens' acropolis.

ATHENS: the biggest and most powerful polis in ancient Greece.

DEMOCRACY: a form of government where the people participate.

LONG WALLS: long stone walls that protected the road between Athens and the port of Piraeus.

MERCHANT SHIP: cargo ships important for trade.

TRIREME: a Greek warship powered by a large crew of oarsmen.

BOW: the front of a boat.

THE FIRST WORLD MAP

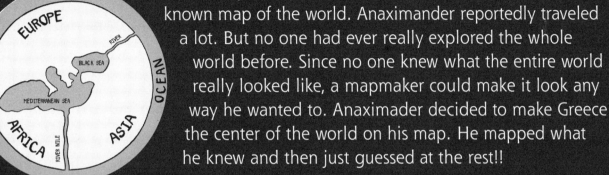

Anaximander of Miletus was a Greek philosopher and astronomer. A philosopher is a great thinker. An astronomer is someone who studies the stars. In the early sixth century, he created a map of the world. It is the first known map of the world. Anaximander reportedly traveled a lot. But no one had ever really explored the whole world before. Since no one knew what the entire world really looked like, a mapmaker could make it look any way he wanted to. Anaximader decided to make Greece the center of the world on his map. He mapped what he knew and then just guessed at the rest!!

The Parthenon is a large, beautiful temple dedicated to the Greek goddess Athena. The whole thing was made out of white marble! It had 46 columns that were over 30 feet tall. You have probably seen pictures of what's left of the Parthenon. The ruins attract thousands of visitors every year. You'll learn more about Athena and the Parthenon later on.

KEEP OUT!

Something that helped Athens survive and thrive were the **Long Walls**. The Long Walls were exactly what they sound like—walls! These parallel stone walls were over 65 feet high. They protected the land between the city of Athens and the port of Piraeus. They were 525 feet apart and over 20,000 feet long. During a time of war, they helped protect Athens from attack while keeping the route to the sea open. A route to the sea was really important because that was where supplies arrived by ship. The Romans destroyed the Long Walls in 86 BCE.

BOATS

You know ancient Greece was a collection of islands. So can you guess how people got around? That's right! They traveled by boat.

Merchant ships were very important in trading. They provided city-states with an easy and cheap way to get goods to and from other areas. These goods included things like olive oil, figs, wine, pottery, spices, and grains. Merchant ships had a simple, rounded design. They were usually less than 100 feet long and very heavy. They looked kind of like big fishing boats with decks. Most had one rectangular sail. When there was little wind crews (sometimes only four of five people) used oars to row through the seas. This was slow going, but even with good winds, these ships weren't fast. Because they were slow, these ships couldn't outrun bad weather or pirates. To stay safe, captains and crews kept their ships close to shore.

Boats that could move quickly through the seas were called **triremes**. Triremes were ancient Greek warships. They were long and made of wood. Instead of using sails to move, these ships used men, lots of men! Up to 200 men would sit on three different levels on each side of the ships' hull and row with oars. The word *triremes* means "three oars." Rowing from the bottom level must have been hot and cramped. But when everyone

JOKE TIME

Q: WHERE DID GREEK SHIPS GO WHEN THEY WERE SICK?

A: TO THE DOC(K)!

COOL *artifact*

Greek sailors painted large eyes on the sides of their ships. Sailors believed these eyes protected a ship from danger.

SPARTA

Sparta was another famous city-state. Like Athens, it was large and powerful and had plenty of good farm land, and early in its history, it was bustling with art, music, and poetry. But then, its neighbors attacked. After this, Sparta decided to concentrate on its military. Soon, Sparta had the strongest military force in ancient Greece. Spartans had a reputation for being fierce warriors. In order to keep its army strong, the government of Sparta made every boy serve in the military. Boys left home when they were seven to begin training. Military training continued until age thirty. Boys were expected to learn how to run, fight, and jump and to be very fit. Even though they didn't serve in the military, Spartan girls also had to be fit. They had to train, too, so they could have healthy and strong babies. This was different from life for girls in Athens. Girls in Athens were kept indoors and didn't do much physical work.

For much of ancient Greek history, Sparta and Athens were enemies. There were times, though, that the two city-states fought together against a common enemy.

was working together, triremes could move about 10 miles per hour. This is about as fast as a human could run if he or she ran at full speed. This helped protect the ships from pirates.

Ancient Greek sailors had another tool to ward off pirates, too. They used rams. Rams are long, wooden poles with metal tips that are used to crash into something else. Greek sailors attached them to the **bows** of the their boats, but the rams were underwater so enemies couldn't see them. The crew of a trireme would run the ram into an approaching pirate ship. This would put a hole in the pirate ship and cause it to sink.

BE AN Archa

An archaeologist is someone who studies objects from the past to learn about ancient people. Archaeologists have learned about ancient Greece by studying things like the writing and everyday objects of that time. We have also learned a lot about ancient Greece by studying Greek art. Ancient Greek pottery was decorated with lots of pictures. Here's a fun way to learn about people by studying some pictures.

SUPPLIES

a box or photo album with old, family photos, especially of your parents when they were kids

notebook

pencil or pen

magnifying glass
(optional)

thin, cloth gloves
(optional)

1 If you have cloth gloves, put them on before starting. Real archaeologists often wear gloves to help protect the objects they are looking at from dirt and fingerprints.

2 Find a place where you have plenty of room to lay out the photos. Use your magnifying glass (if you have one) to study the photos closely. Record your observations in your notebook just like a real archaeologist. Make a guess at what year the photo was taken and who is in the picture.

eologist

Ask yourself:
- ◈ What can I tell about the people in the photos?
- ◈ What kind of clothes are they wearing?
- ◈ What season is it?
- ◈ What are the people doing?
- ◈ Are they having fun?

 After you've made some guesses, ask your parents or grandparents what they know about the photos.

4 When you're done, make sure you put away all the photos carefully. A real archaeologist would never leave artifacts lying out.

THEN & NOW

 **THEN:** Athens was the biggest and most important city-state in ancient Greece.

NOW: Athens is the capital of modern Greece.

MAKE A Sailboat

1 Use one or two staples to staple the Post-it Notes together. Put the staples along the side where the sticky part is.

2 On the first page, draw a simple Greek sailboat close to the left side. Remember, Greek sailboats had square sails. You can also draw a Greek warship if you'd like. Put your sailboat in some water or draw a shore nearby. Since you'll be drawing your scene 20 times, don't get too detailed or it will take you a long time!

3 On the second page, draw your boat a little over to the right side. On each of the following pages, draw your boat a little farther right. You can change your background, too. For example, make the sun rise and set. Do this by drawing the sun a little higher in the sky each time. You could also add rolling waves.

4 When you're done, flip the pages from front to back quickly to watch your boat sail across the page!

SUPPLIES

20 Post-it Notes— don't pull them apart

stapler

colored markers

Play Pirates
ARE COMING!

The object of this game is to sneak up and tag the captain before you get caught, or rammed.

1 Choose one person to be captain. All the other players are pirates. Pirates line up arms-length apart at one end of the play area.

2 The captain stands at the other end of the play area, facing the pirates. First the captain calls "sail!" and turns so his or her back is to the pirates. While the captain's back is turned, the pirates try to sneak up on the captain as quickly as they can.

SUPPLIES

4 or more people

large area to run around in

3 After a few moments, the captain turns around and calls "pirate!" The pirates have to freeze. Any pirate the captain catches moving must go back to the starting point. Then the captain turns back around, calls "sail!" and the game continues.

4 If the captain turns around and calls, "ram!" instead of "pirate" any pirate caught moving is considered sunk and must sit down for the rest of the game. A captain can call "ram," no more than three times during a game. The game goes on until all pirates are sunk or until one pirate sneaks up and tags the captain from behind. That pirate becomes the new captain.

WELCOME HOME!

ncient Greeks are known for their large, beautiful buildings. You might think they lived in fancy homes, too. But guess what? Their homes were usually pretty plain and simple. Ancient Greek houses were made from mudbricks. To make these bricks, ancient Greeks mixed mud, straw, and pebbles. Then they poured the mixture into molds and let the sun dry it. Mudbricks were easy and cheap to make, but they had their problems, too.

THEN & NOW

THEN: Ancient Greeks had a statue of the god Hermes in front of their homes to ward off evil.

NOW: Some Greek people wear or decorate their homes with evil eye charms. These charms are the image of an eye set in a blue stone.

They didn't last long and tended to crumble. This meant that homeowners had to make repairs often. Roofs were made from baked ceramic tiles, and foundations were made from stone.

The streets in Athens were narrow. Houses were close together, were one or two stories high, and they didn't have yards. From the outside, most homes looked alike. They had high, small, shuttered windows and were painted plain colors such as white or tan. The only decoration outside a house was a small stand with a bust of the god Hermes. Ancient Greeks believed Hermes kept evil from entering a house.

The insides of Greek houses were a little more interesting. The rooms were centered around an open-roofed area called a **courtyard**. The sun shone into the courtyard, which often contained plants and fountains. Families liked to hang out around the courtyard and the nearby covered area called the exedra (kind of a covered porch).

The main area of the house was used for entertaining. This room was called the **andron**. It was like a dining room or banquet room. Greek men gathered here to eat and socialize. Mosaics, or designs made of ceramic tile, often covered the floor of this room.

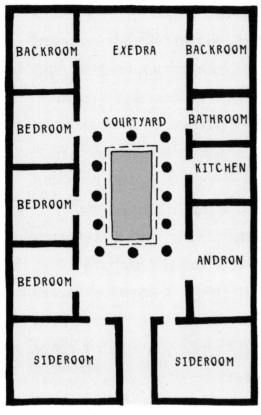

Next to the andron was the kitchen, and near the kitchen was the bathroom. Inside the bathroom was a basin and a small, ceramic bathtub. Wealthy homes even had a simple shower system sometimes. (Ancient Greeks prided themselves on being clean.) People went to the bathroom in chamber pots that were then emptied into the streets. The rest of the rooms surrounding the courtyard were bedrooms. Some houses had only one or two bedrooms. Other houses, such as those in the country or those that belonged to the rich, had up to ten bedrooms.

Ancient Greek homes had front doors to keep out intruders. But inside, instead of doors, rooms had curtains to separate them from other areas of the house. Walls were decorated with pictures painted on wooden panels. Often, ancient Greeks painted at least one wall a bright color. Dark red was a popular choice. Some families decorated walls with painted borders.

OIKOS

Ancient Greeks didn't use the word *family*. The household, including family members and slaves, was called the **oikos**. The male head of the *oikos* was completely in charge of everyone who lived in his house. Everyone had to obey him.

"NO GIRLS ALLOWED"

In ancient Greece, men and women spent their time in different parts of the home. The men's area of the house was called the **andronitis**. This is where men met

WORDS to KNOW

COURTYARD: the small open-roofed area in the center of an ancient Greek home.

ANDRON: the area of a Greek home where the men would entertain guests and hold dinner parties.

OIKOS: everyone who was part of an ancient Greek household.

ANDRONITIS: the men's area of an ancient Greek home.

GYNAECONITIS: the women's area of an ancient Greek home.

THALAMOS: the master bedroom of an ancient Greek home.

visitors, exercised, or just hung out. Only grown men or male slaves were allowed in this part of the house. If the house had two stories, the andronitis was on the first floor. If the house had only one story, the andronitis was on one side of the house.

The women's area of a home was called the **gynaeconitis**. This is where all the female family members, female slaves, and boys under age six spent their time. Wealthy ancient Greeks believed women should be protected from the outside world. So women of wealthier families spent most of their time at home. They ran the household,

took care of the children, and managed the money. They did the cooking and cleaning or oversaw the slaves who did those things. They also spun the wool and sewed all the clothes. In addition to doing household work, poor women often worked outside the home alongside their husbands at shops and in the fields.

COOL artifact

Ancient Greek parents usually arranged marriages for their children. When a man and a woman married, the woman's family gave the man a dowry. A dowry is the money (or gifts) a man receives from his wife's family in exchange for taking care of her in marriage.

JOKE TIME

Q: WHAT DID THE ANCIENT GREEK CHILD CALL HIS THREE-LEGGED CHAIR?

A: A COOL STOOL

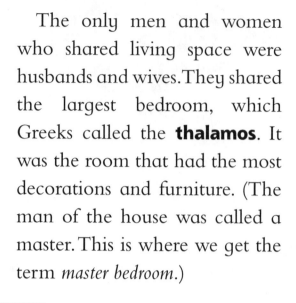

The only men and women who shared living space were husbands and wives. They shared the largest bedroom, which Greeks called the **thalamos**. It was the room that had the most decorations and furniture. (The man of the house was called a master. This is where we get the term *master bedroom*.)

FURNITURE

Ancient Greeks, both rich and poor, had little furniture. Tables were usually round. Some had three legs. Others had four legs. People sat on wooden chairs or stools. Furniture was often moved from room to room as needed. The master of the house had a special chair called a *thronos*. It had arms and a padded seat. Couches and beds had wooden frames and leather webbing. Ancient Greeks used shelves, baskets, and earthenware vases for storage. They also used wooden chests to store things. Small stoves called braziers heated their houses. And oil lamps gave light.

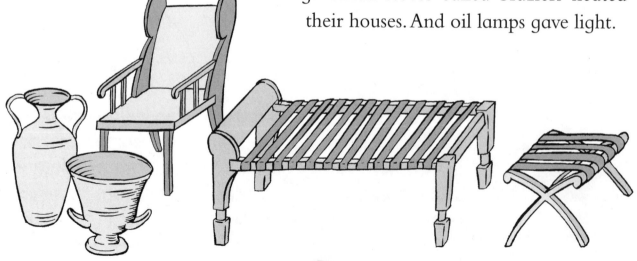

MAKE A MODEL OF AN
Oil Lamp

This is only a pretend lamp. Don't ever try to light it. Real ancient Greek oil lamps were made out of terra cotta, bronze, or silver. Look for dark red, bronze, or silver paint at the craft or hardware store.

1 Cover your work area in wax paper. Mold most of your clay into a shallow bowl shape about 6 inches in diameter. This will be your lamp.

2 Roll a medium-sized piece of clay into a log about as thick as your finger and 5 inches long. Gently curve the log into a "C" shape for the lamp's handle. Attach the handle to the lamp.

3 Cut out two flame-shaped pieces of orange paper for your lamp's flames. Glue the skinny end of the toothpick between the pieces of paper for your lamp's wick.

4 Poke the toothpick into the center of your oil lamp. You can use small bits of leftover clay to decorate the edge of the lamp or the handle. Let the clay dry. When your oil lamp is hard, you can paint it.

SUPPLIES

wax paper

air-hardening clay

orange construction paper

scissors

toothpick

glue

craft paint

MAKE A
Courtyard

SUPPLIES

newspaper

empty toilet paper roll

cardboard

pencil

scissors

paint brush

gold paint

black paint

paper towel

white paint

toothpick

glue

1 Cover your workspace with newspaper. Stand the toilet paper roll on top of the cardboard. Carefully draw two matching circles that are slightly bigger than the end of the paper roll. Cut the circles out with the scissors.

2 Paint the tops and bottoms of the cardboard circles gold. Set them aside. Paint the outside of the paper roll black. Let it dry for a few minutes.

3 Crumple up the paper towel and dip it into a small bit of white paint. Dab the white paint all over the black paint to create a marbled effect. Let the white paint dry for a few minutes.

Column

4 Dip the end of the toothpick in white paint. Drag the toothpick along the column to make skinny lines. These lines should run parallel to each other and at an angle. Don't worry if they aren't exactly the same. It looks more realistic if they aren't! These lines will be the marble's veins.

5 Dab a corner of the paper towel (or your finger) along the white veins to lightly blend the paint. Allow the the paint to dry. This is your column.

6 When the paint is dry, glue the gold pieces to the top and bottom of the column. Now you have a miniature marble column that looks like the ones ancient Greeks had in their courtyards!

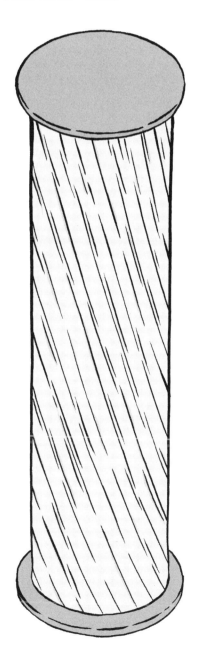

WEAVE A Basket

You'll be using sharp scissors for this project. Ask an adult for help.

1 Carefully cut 11 slits in the side of the container from the top to the bottom. Don't cut the bottom. The slits should be about 1½ inches apart. You'll have 11 flaps when you're done. You can use a different container, just make sure you have an odd number of flaps.

2 Tie a knot about 6 inches from the end of your ball of yarn. Slide the yarn between two of the flaps. Pull the knot down until it is near the bottom of the container. The knot and extra yarn should be inside the container.

3 Start weaving! Wrap the yarn in front of one flap. Then wrap the yarn behind the next flap. Keep wrapping the yarn in front of one flap and behind the next one, all the way around the container.

4 Keep wrapping the yarn. Be careful not to skip any flaps. Gently push the yarn down as you go. This will make your weave nice and even.

5 Stop weaving when you get to the lip of the container. Cut the yarn, leaving a few extra inches. Tie this end of the yarn to the 6-inch piece at the bottom of the container, then cut off any extra lengths of yarn. You can use your basket to hold small items, such as coins or jewelry.

SUPPLIES

8-ounce Cool Whip plastic container

scissors

ball of yarn, any color

LET'S EAT!

Many ancient Greeks shared similar diets. It didn't matter if they were rich or poor. (Of course, the rich enjoyed some foods that the poor couldn't. For example, they ate meat more often.) Breakfast was usually simple, often a piece of bread and some wine. Lunch may have been just bread and a piece of cheese or fruit. Dinner was the main meal of the day. It included bread, cheese, fruits, vegetables, and wine.

ICE COLD

In some ways ancient Greeks were a lot like us. They enjoyed nice cold drinks on hot days. They didn't have refrigerators, though. To keep their drinks cold, they put them in special vessels underground. That's because it's cooler underground. If they could afford it, they also had someone haul ice down from the mountains. Since there was no way to keep extra ice, people had to fetch new ice every day.

Many of the people who lived around Athens were farmers. The valleys and the land around the coasts made good farmland with rich soil. Farmers grew all kinds of crops. Any food they didn't need for their household, they sold at the market in the town square, called the **agora**. Farmers grew all kinds of crops: grapes, figs, lettuce, garlic, carrots, leeks, cucumbers, artichokes, beets, lentils, peas, onions, and cabbage.

In preparing food, ancient Greeks used spices, such as cinnamon and cloves, and sweeteners, such as honey. They also used a bad-smelling sauce made from old fish, called *garos*, to flavor foods. Ancient Romans used this sauce, too, but they called it *garum*.

Wheat and barley were always important crops, too. Ancient Greeks used them to make bread and a watery porridge. Bread was served at all meals. People used bread to soak up sauces or scoop up food. Did you know that ancient Greeks didn't use

COOL *artifact*

Merchants who sold meat or fish in stalls at the market had a problem. The hot sun spoiled the meat. Their solution was to put the meat and fish on marble slabs. These kept the meat cool.

forks or spoons to eat? They ate with their fingers. Women cooked on grills over open fires or in small clay ovens.

In addition to growing crops, farmers kept animals. They used oxen to help plow the soil. They also had sheep, goats, and poultry. Most animals weren't used for meat, though. Farmers kept them for milk or eggs. Ancient Greeks, especially poor ancient Greeks, didn't eat meat very often. In fact, the only time many ancient Greeks ate meat was when an animal was sacrificed to honor a god. Then the meat was shared with the community. Most Greeks ate lots of fish, though.

OLIVES AND GRAPES

Olives and grapes were the most important crops in ancient Greece. Olive groves thrived there. People used olives for lots of things. They ate olives, of course. But they also pressed olives to remove the oil. The oil was used in cooking, as fuel for lamps, and as a kind of soap. Olive oil was also important in makeup and medicine, too. Ancient Greeks sold their olives and olive oil to other countries, too.

The ancient Greeks used grapes to make wine. Wine was a big part of their daily and spiritual lives. They took wine making very seriously. Every year, the ancient Greeks held celebrations in honor of **Dionysos**,

JOKE TIME

KNOCK, KNOCK.
WHO'S THERE?
OLIVE.
OLIVE WHO?
OLIVE IT WHEN YOU
GET MY JOKES!

the god of wine. When the grapes were ready in the fall, the ancient Greeks put them into big tubs. Workers stomped on the grapes with their bare feet! Then the juice was left to **ferment** in goatskin containers.

Everyone drank wine and it was served with most meals. Wine makers put water in the wine, though. The water diluted the syrupy wine. Ancient Greek wine was about one part wine and two parts water. It was considered uncivilized to drink wine that wasn't watered down. It was also highly unacceptable to be drunk in public.

Like olives and olive oil, ancient Greeks sold wine to nearby countries. They bottled the wine in rounded, clay containers with skinny necks called **amphorae**. Selling wine was big business in ancient Greece.

THEN & NOW

THEN: Greeks enjoyed baklava, a sweet dessert made with thin sheets of pastry, nuts, and honey.

NOW: Baklava is still a popular, sweet treat in Greece.

couches called **klines**. Slaves placed small tables in front of the klines. Guests ate while they stretched out and leaned on one arm.

Food at these parties was plentiful and fancy. There were a variety of breads, cheeses, vegetables, and fish. For dessert, partygoers dined on fruit and cakes and a sweet dish called baklava. There were often musicians, dancers, and acrobats to entertain guests. After the eating and music were finished, guests drank wine, discussed serious topics like politics and philosophy, recited poetry, or sang hymns. These lively exchanges were called **symposiums**.

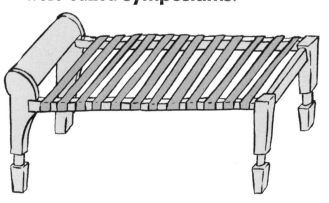

THE DINNER PARTY

Wealthy ancient Greeks liked to throw fancy dinner parties. These parties were strictly men only. Guests were led to the dining room and invited to lie on long

WORDS to KNOW

AGORA: the open marketplace in the middle of an ancient Greek town.

DIONYSOS: the god of wine.

FERMENT: when a substance breaks down over time into another sub stance, such as grape juice turning into wine.

AMPHORAE: rounded clay containers with long necks that the ancient Greeks put olive oil and wine in.

KLINES: long couches that were used at ancient Greek dinner parties. Guests ate lying down.

SYMPOSIUM: a party at which ancient Greek men would drink, sing, and discuss politics and philosophy.

KYLIX: a shallow, two-handled cup used for drinking wine.

VESSELS AND VASES

Ancient Greeks are famous for their beautiful pottery. Vases and vessels were useful, but they were also works of art. Potters worked on pottery wheels in special quarters called *keramikos*. They baked the clay in ovens called kilns. Greek pottery is usually known as "black figure" or "red figure." Black-figure pottery had red backgrounds with black figures. Red-figure pottery had black backgrounds with red figures.

Greek vases and vessels were decorated with detailed paintings. Even the insides of many bowls, cups, and vases had pictures. These scenes showed daily life, hunts, gods, and festivals. Much of what we know about ancient Greek life we learned by studying these vases. In later years, Greek vases were decorated with designs inspired by the art of the Orient.

Vases and vessels came in many shapes and sizes, depending on what they were used for. For example, ancient Greeks used cups carved into the shapes of animal heads, called rhytons, to share drinks of wine. Because of the way it was designed, the cup couldn't be put down without spilling the drink! They also drank wine from shallow two-handled cups called **kylix**. And, as you probably remember, amphorae held oil and wine. Other kinds of vessels held makeup and perfume.

Just like olives and wine, Greek pottery was very popular in other countries. The ancient Greeks sold and traded a lot of their pottery.

HOST A Symposium

Hosting your own symposium is easy and fun!

SUPPLIES

pillows

plates

snack foods (bread, fruit, vegetables)

cups

white grape juice

1 Invite some friends over. Ancient Greek symposiums were strictly for men, but you can have both boys and girls.

2 Lay some pillows on the floor to make your own version of a *kline* for each guest. Your guests can remove their shoes and lie on their sides.

3 Place plates of bite-size food in front of your guests and have everyone eat with their fingers. You can serve a variety of breads, fruits, and vegetables, or even make a Greek salad.

4 Serve white grape juice with the food. Be sure to ask if this is okay with your parents first. White grape juice won't stain as badly as red grape juice, but you should still be careful.

5 Listen to music, tell jokes or stories, and discuss important (or funny) issues while you eat. After the meal you can play musical instruments.

MAKE A Kylix

A kylix is a two-handled cup the ancient Greeks used. When they weren't drinking from it, the family hung the cup on the wall, by one of the handles, for decoration.

1 Spread the newspaper over your workspace. Set the plastic container's lid off to one side for the moment. Carefully cut the container in half so the bottom half makes a shallow cup.

2 From the top piece of plastic that's left, cut two pieces that are 6 inches long and about ¾ inches wide.

3 Bend the pieces of plastic to create handles. Using the masking tape, attach the handles (one on each side) to the shallow cup.

4 Cut the paper towel roll in half. This will be the "stem" of your cup. Tape one end to the bottom of the cup.

5 Now, tape the other end of the stem onto the plastic container's lid. The lid will be the base of your *kylix*.

6 Cut the plaster cloth into small pieces, each about the size of a playing card. One at a time, dip the pieces of plaster cloth into the water and begin laying them on the cup. Cover the whole cup (including the handles, stem, and base) in several layers of plaster cloth. Smooth out any bumps with your wet fingers.

7 Let the cup dry completely. When it's done, paint it with a coat of the reddish-brown paint.

8 Once the paint is dry, you can paint a scene or add designs using the black paint. You can't really drink out of your *kylix*, but you can have fun pretending! You can also hang your cup up for display if you'd like.

SUPPLIES

newspaper

clean and dry 8-ounce plastic container with lid

scissors

masking tape

empty paper towel roll

plaster cloth, sometimes called plaster gauze, found with the plaster of Paris at craft stores— Rigid Wrap is one brand

shallow bowl of water

paint brush

reddish-brown paint

black paint

MAKE A Greek Salad

This recipe uses feta cheese, made from goat's milk. (The ancient Greeks didn't have cows.) You'll be using a sharp knife, so ask an adult for help.

1 Cut the tomatoes and cucumber into cubes. Put them into the mixing bowl.

2 Cut the red onion into thin rings. Add them to the bowl. Cut the seeds out of the pepper. Then cut the pepper into long, thin strips or cubes. Add the pepper pieces to the bowl, too.

3 Next, add the olives to the bowl. Sprinkle the olive oil, vinegar, oregano, salt, and pepper over all the items in the bowl. Gently toss all the ingredients together.

4 Finally, add the feta to the salad and gently toss the ingredients again. Now, your Greek salad is ready to eat. Yum!

SUPPLIES

- cutting board
- sharp knife
- 2 red tomatoes
- 1 small cucumber
- mixing bowl
- 1 small red onion
- 1 small bell pepper (green, red or a little of both)
- ½ cup pitted, black olives
- 2 tablespoons olive oil
- 1 tablespoon red wine vinegar
- ½ teaspoon oregano
- salt and pepper to taste
- ½ cup crumbled feta cheese

CLOTHES

Ancient Greeks took a lot of pride in how they looked. They believed a person should look his or her best at all times. While their clothes were fairly simple, that didn't mean the clothes weren't beautiful. Ancient Greek clothes were also practical. Most clothes were made of lightweight fabric because it was so sunny and hot. Sometimes the cloth was so lightweight that you could see through it. It's a good thing ancient Greeks weren't shy about their bodies!

FANCY WOMEN

Ancient Greek women wore lots of beautiful jewelry. Rings, brooches, bracelets, necklaces, and earrings were popular. These items were often made of gold and silver. They were usually big and fancy, as well. Women also wore makeup. They used powder to make their skin look paler. Remember, pale skin was considered pretty. Women kept their makeup in a round pot called a pyxis.

Men and women wore the same piece of clothing. It was called a **chiton**. A chiton was made from a rectangular piece of material cut into two pieces. The two pieces were then fastened at intervals across the shoulders and arms. Wearers put on chitons by pulling them over their heads (like you'd put on a shirt) and then wrapped a belt around their waist. Chitons looked kind of like a loose sleeveless dress.

Women wore chitons that went down to their ankles. Men wore chitons that went to their knees. Can you think of a reason why women and men wore chitons that were different lengths? If you said men usually worked at jobs in which they needed to move around more, you're right! Men sometimes wore longer chitons for parties or formal business, though. Ancient Greek children also wore knee-length chitons. They needed clothes that let them run around and move easily.

WORDS to KNOW

CHITON: a piece of clothing that men and women wore in ancient Greek times.

BROOCH: a special pin.

HIMATION: a large piece of material that the ancient Greeks wore over their shoulders.

CHLAMYS: a short cloak worn by ancient Greeks.

PETASOS: a flat, wide-brimmed hat that ancient Greeks wore.

THEN & NOW

THEN: The hot weather affected how ancient Greeks dressed and lived.

NOW: Some Greeks take naps during the hottest part of the day to avoid the heat.

Though everyone wore the same basic piece of clothing, the accessories and fabric colors were different. Some ancient Greeks fastened their chitons with simple buttons. Other people used fancy **brooches** or pins made of ivory or gold. If you were poor, your chiton was white. The rich could afford to have their clothes brightly dyed. Chitons were often dyed shades of red or purple.

Sometimes, people wore belts to jazz things up. **Himations** added flash, too. They also added warmth. A himation was a large rectangular piece of material. Women draped them around their shoulders like shawls. Men often just draped them over one shoulder. A **chlamys** was a shorter version of a himation. They were the ancient Greek version of a jacket.

People sold clothes at the agora. But most ancient Greeks made their own clothes at home.

KEEPING COOL IN THE HOT SUN

Ancient Greek weather was hot. It was important for people to protect themselves from the sun. Ancient Greek men wore a hat called a **petasos**. It was made of felt and was round

COOL
artifact

Ancient Greeks bathed in small bathtubs. They also got clean by rubbing oil on their skin, then scraping the oil (and the dirt) off.

and flat. It had a wide brim to keep the sun off of the wearer's face. When women went out, they often wore veils to protect their heads and faces from the sun. Ancient Greeks thought suntans were unattractive. Pale skin meant you were wealthy enough that you didn't have to work outdoors.

Men kept their hair short. They didn't usually have beards or mustaches. Long hair was the fashion for women. It was often pulled up or braided, though. (It was probably a lot cooler this way.) Women used beautiful headbands, nets, ribbons, and hairpins to keep their hair in place.

Ancient Greeks also needed to protect their feet from the hot ground. When they were indoors, ancient Greeks went barefoot. But when they went outdoors, they wore leather sandals. These sandals had laces that wrapped around a person's ankles or legs. Workers and soldiers wore leather boots. Ancient Greeks didn't like wearing shoes, though. They tried to avoid it if they could.

JOKE TIME

Q: WHAT'S ANOTHER NAME FOR A PETASOS?

A: A FLAT HAT!

MAKE A Chiton

You can sew or glue your chiton together. If you sew it, be sure to ask an adult to help.

1 Lay the pieces of material on top of each other. Along the top edge, mark an opening for your head about 11 inches wide.

2 Sew or glue the rest of the top edges at intervals a few inches apart. Sew or glue the buttons at the intervals along the top edges.

3 Pull the chiton over your head. Wrap the cord around your waist. Pull the chiton up and over the belt until it's the length you want it to be. Or you could shorten it by cutting extra material from the bottom edge. Now you're ready to step out in ancient Greek style!

SUPPLIES

2 rectangular pieces of linen or cotton material, each as wide as your outstretched arms and as long as the distance from your shoulders to your ankles

pencil

ruler

sewing machine OR glue

needle and thread OR glue

10 buttons (shiny ones would look really cool!)

scissors

piece of cord for a belt

MAKE A Brooch

You'll be using spray paint for this project. Ask a grown-up to help. If you don't have a self-sticking pin, you can use a safety pin. Just attach it to the back of your brooch with masking tape.

SUPPLIES

newspaper

small plastic lid, such as the lid of a Pringles can

scissors

fabric paint, any color

gold or silver spray paint

self-sticking brooch pin found in the jewelry-making aisle at a craft store

1 Spread the newspaper over your work area. Cut off the edge of the lid. Next, cut the lid to the size you'd like your brooch to be.

2 Use the fabric paint to draw a design on the lid. Ancient Greeks often used geometric designs or faces to decorate their jewelry. Let the fabric paint dry completely before going to the next step.

3 When the fabric paint is dry, follow the directions on the spray-paint can to paint the lid. You can paint both sides if you'd like. Let the spray paint dry.

4 Finally, add the self-sticking pin to the back of your brooch. You can wear your new brooch on your chiton!

MAKE A Foot Scrub

Ancient Greeks used olive oil to clean and protect their skin. A foot scrub is a great way to sooth tired feet after going barefoot all day. This recipe makes enough for one treatment. Because it uses olive oil, you can't save it. It will go bad.

SUPPLIES

small mixing bowl

2 tablespoons light olive oil

5 drops peppermint, spearmint, or wintergreen essential oil found in the soap-making section of a craft store

1 tablespoon sea salt
(optional)

spoon

1 Mix the olive oil and the essential oil in your bowl. Add the salt. Salt will help scrub off dirt and dead skin. It makes the foot rub a little rough.

2 To use your foot rub, sit on the edge of the bathtub. Rub the oil all over your bare feet until they are clean and relaxed. When you're done, rinse your feet with warm, soapy water. Dry your tootsies, and you're ready to go! Just be careful not to slip.

SCHOOL, SOCRATES, and SCIENCE

Ancient Greeks believed that education was very important. Just like children today, ancient Greek children had lessons. They didn't have school buildings, though. Instead, children went to "school" at a teacher's house or at a pubic place like a market. Learning took place from dawn until dusk. Families often hired someone to follow a student to make sure he behaved and worked hard!

In ancient Greece, girls did not go to school. Their mothers taught them at home. They learned how to sew, weave, cook, and do other household chores. However, some wealthy families hired tutors to teach their girls to read and write.

Poor boys also learned at home. Sometimes they became apprentices to learn a trade. An apprentice helps a shopkeeper or artist and learns that person's job. If his family could afford it, a boy started school when he was about seven. Sometimes boys had school in one place, with different teachers to teach them. Other times, boys went to different places to learn the different subjects. It all depended on what a family wanted to do or could afford.

Younger students (age seven to ten) learned how to read and write. The teacher who taught these subjects was called a *grammatistes*. Students didn't have textbooks or calculators like they do today. They read from scrolls, or long rolls of **papyrus**. Papyrus is a kind of paper made from the papyrus plant. To do math calculations, they used a counter called an **abacus**.

GREEK LETTERS

The Greek alphabet has 24 letters. It is based on the alphabet of the Phoenicians, people who were neighbors of the ancient Greeks. It's considered the first, real alphabet because it was the first to use symbols for each vowel and consonant sound. The ancient alphabet is still used in modern-day Greece. Many of the Greek letters are used in science and mathematics, too. For example, mathematicians often use letters from the Greek alphabet to represent numbers.

A	B	Γ	Δ	E	Z
ALPHA	BETA	GAMMA	DELTA	EPSILON	ZETA
H	Θ	I	K	Λ	M
ETA	THETA	IOTA	KAPPA	LAMBDA	MU
N	Ξ	O	Π	P	Σ
NU	XI	OMICRON	PI	RHO	SIGMA
T	Y	Φ	X	Ψ	Ω
TAU	UPSILON	PHI	CHI	PSI	OMEGA

WORDS to KNOW

PAPYRUS: paper made from pressing a reed plant that is also called papyrus.

ABACUS: a counting tool made with beads strung on wires that the ancient Greeks used to solve math problems.

DEBATE: to argue about something, trying to convince the other person of a point of view.

An abacus had beads strung along several wires to help with advanced counting. Along with reading, writing, and math, ancient Greek boys learned how to speak in public and to **debate**. Some of their lessons included poetry. They had to memorize poems or parts of poems and recite them by heart.

From about age ten to twelve, boys learned to play an instrument. The teacher who taught music was called a *kitharistes*. Being able to sing and play music was considered an important part of being an educated person. One of the most popular instruments in ancient Greece was the lyre. A lyre looks kind of like a miniature harp. It was made using a turtle shell, wooden bows, and three to seven strings for strumming. A musician often played a lyre while reciting poetry or singing. Drums, finger cymbals, and pipes called *aulos* (kind of like clarinets or oboes) were also popular.

From about age twelve to eighteen, physical education took up most of a student's time. The reason for this is simple. In ancient Greece, a good citizen was someone who could be a good soldier. And to be a good soldier, a boy had to be physically fit. The special gym boys went to was called a *palaistra*. A teacher called a *paidotribes* led boys in sports. Ancient Greek boys learned to wrestle, box, run, and throw the discus.

COOL artifact

Ancient Greek students wrote on a wooden tablet that was covered in wax. They etched their letters and numbers into the wax using a long stick called a stylus. The stylus had a flat end to rub out mistakes.

SCIENCE AND MATH

Education was important to the ancient Greeks. It shouldn't come as a surprise that they made many advances in math and science. For example, ancient Greeks were among the first to map the world and the stars. They suggested that the earth was a sphere, like a ball. They were also the first to think that the sun was a ball of fire and that the earth moved around it. They explored the idea of atoms and built many useful machines. They also discovered mathematical formulas that we still use. Three important scientists from ancient Greece are Hippocrates, Pythagoras, and Archimedes.

$\pi = 3.14159265358\ldots$

$$a^2 + b^2 = c^2$$

Hippocrates was a doctor. In ancient Greece, doctors weren't experts like they are today. They didn't know a lot about how the body works. Unlike many doctors of the time, Hippocrates asked his patients a lot of questions. He kept track of their symptoms and past illnesses. This made it easier to treat them. He also helped to write many medical books. These books told other doctors what to look for and how to treat illnesses.

ANCIENT GREEK STORIES

Some of the poems from ancient Greece are quite famous. A writer named **Homer** wrote two of them. These poems are called *The Iliad* and *The Odyssey*. *The Iliad* retells the story of the Trojan War. *The Odyssey* tells the story of Odysseus, a war hero, and his journey home from the Trojan War. *The Odyssey* has over 12,000 lines. And *The Iliad* has over 15,000 lines!

AHA!

$a^2 + b^2 = c^2$, MY THEOREM!

Because of all his work, Hippocrates is known as the father of medicine. Today, new doctors take a pledge to do their best and treat patients kindly. This is known as the Hippocratic Oath. You can probably guess who it's named after!

Pythagoras was one of the first mathematicians. He studied numbers and patterns. He thought that many things could be explained with numbers. Some of his greatest discoveries had to do with triangles. He didn't discover triangles, of course. He just noticed some interesting things about them. For instance, he discovered that the sum of a triangle's angles equaled 180 degrees.

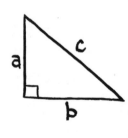

THE HIPPOCRATIC OATH
(WELL, PART OF IT, AT LEAST)

...I will prescribe regimens for the good of my patients according to my ability and my judgment and never do harm to anyone...
If I keep this oath faithfully, may I enjoy my life and practice my art, respected by all men and in all times...

He also discovered a formula for figuring out how long the sides of a right triangle are. A right triangle is a triangle with a right angle in it. The formula is even named after him: the Pythagorean theorem.

Archimedes was a mathematician and inventor. One of his useful inventions was called the Archimedes screw. It was a simple machine that used a turning motion to move water from one place to another. It helped farmers water their crops. He also calculated a special number to figure out the relationship between the distance around a circle (its circumference) and the distance across the circle through the middle (its diameter). The number is represented this way: π. We call this **pi**. The number goes on forever. To make things easier, we often just use the first few digits and write it like this: 3.14.

JOKE TIME

Q: WHY WAS THE MATH SCROLL STRESSED OUT?

A: IT HAD TOO MANY PROBLEMS.

$$\pi = 3.14159265358...$$

PHILOSOPHY

Wisdom is knowledge that helps you make good decisions. Ancient Greeks were very interested in wisdom. The search for wisdom is called **philosophy**. Someone who searches for wisdom by learning and thinking about things is called a philosopher. Philosophers think about big ideas. For example, they wonder about right and wrong. They wonder about beauty, religion, and nature. Ancient Greece is known for its philosophers, especially Socrates, Plato, and Aristotle.

WORDS to KNOW

HOMER: a famous ancient Greek poet who wrote *The Iliad* and *The Odyssey*.

PI: The irrational number represented by the symbol π and often shortened to 3.14.

PHILOSOPHY: the love of and search for wisdom.

FUN AND GAMES

Ancient Greek children didn't spend all of their time studying. They played, too! Many of the toys they had were like the toys we have today. They played with balls, hoops that they rolled along the ground, tops, dolls made of clay, yo-yos, and models of animals. They also had board games like backgammon and chess. Girls often played knucklebones, which is a lot like the game of Jacks.

When children became teenagers, they were considered grown up. To show they had really left behind their childhoods, they had to give away all their toys to the god Apollo and the goddess Artemis.

Socrates was a teacher. He believed knowledge should be free. He didn't charge for teaching. Socrates loved to challenge his students. He would ask a question, hear the response, then keep asking questions and hearing responses until the student discovered he was wrong. For example, someone might have said, "The sky is always blue." And Socrates might have asked, "What about when it rains?" or "What about at night?"

Socrates had many followers. He also had some enemies. Athens' leaders were upset with Socrates because they thought he didn't respect the gods. When he was seventy, Socrates was thrown in jail for teaching.

Plato was one of Socrates's followers. After Socrates died, Plato wrote down Socrates's ideas and the conversations the two of them had.

THEN & NOW

THEN: Students studied Homer's poems.

NOW: Many students still read and study Homer's *The Iliad* and *The Odyssey*.

Socrates didn't write anything himself, so we know about Socrates from Plato. Thanks, Plato!

Plato was interested in learning about what makes people do the things they do. He also wondered if something is real only because we believe it's real.

Aristotle was one of Plato's students. He used philosophy to study nature and how the world worked. His greatest contribution was his practical method of figuring things out. Because of this, Aristotle is known as the father of the scientific method. This is what Aristotle did:

Step 1: Figure out what you want to know.

Step 2: Form an idea or prediction. This is called a hypothesis.

Step 3: Create and carry out an experiment to test your hypothesis.

Step 4: Collect the information from the experiment.

Step 5: Make a conclusion. Ask, "Was my hypothesis right or wrong?"

SOCRATES' FREE THINKING SCHOOL

MAKE AN
Archimedes

SUPPLIES

- oven
- baking sheet
- cooking spray
- 18 ounces refrigerated cookie dough (you will need only half of the roll but you can save the rest for later)
- small mixing bowl
- spoon
- 4 ounces of cream cheese, softened
- 4 ounces of whipped topping, thawed
- 4 different kinds of sliced fruit, such as strawberries, blueberries, kiwi, grapes, bananas
- knife

Pi is an important mathematical number. Here's a fun and delicious way to remember it by making a real pie! You'll be using the oven and a sharp knife for this project. Ask an adult for help.

1 Preheat your oven to 350 degrees Fahrenheit. Spray your baking sheet with the cooking spray. Use half of the cookie dough to make a circle about 6 inches in diameter on the baking sheet.

$$\pi = 3.14$$

Pi(e)

4 Top the cookie crust with slices of fruit. You can sprinkle the fruit slices all around or arrange them in a design. Get creative!

5 Cut the cookie into three equal pieces. The easiest way to do this is to make a Y shape. When you're done, you'll have a dessert that represents Archimedes's pi: 3 pieces, 1 layer of frosting; and 4 toppings. Yum! Be sure to store any leftovers in the refrigerator.

2 Bake the cookie dough for 10 to 12 minutes or until it's golden brown. Let this cookie dough crust cool completely before going to the next step.

3 In the bowl, mix together the cream cheese and whipped topping. Spread the mixture on top of the cooled cookie crust.

MAKE A
Poetry Scroll

Ancient Greeks who read poetry out loud to entertain others were called bards. Once you finish this project you can dress up in a chiton and be a bard yourself.

1 Cover your work space with newspaper. You will also need to lay out some newspapers so you will have space for your project to dry.

2 Place the three pieces of white paper into the baking sheet or shallow tray. Slowly pour the cold coffee or tea over the paper. Let the paper soak for five minutes.

3 Carefully lift each piece of paper, letting the extra liquid drip off. Lay the sheets to dry on some newspaper. Do not stack them.

4 When the sheets of paper are completely dry, tape them together lengthwise. Your papyrus poetry scroll is almost finished! Write your poem on the middle page.

5 Roll in the top and bottom sheets of papyrus. When you're done, your paper will look like an ancient Greek scroll. To recite your poem, gently unroll the scroll and start reading!

SUPPLIES

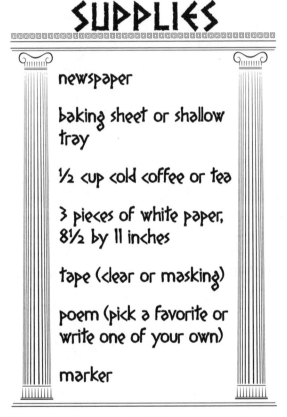

newspaper

baking sheet or shallow tray

½ cup cold coffee or tea

3 pieces of white paper, 8½ by 11 inches

tape (clear or masking)

poem (pick a favorite or write one of your own)

marker

Play Morra

Morra is a game children and grown-ups in ancient Greece played. Many people still play Morra. There are lots of variations on the game. In this version, players must count quickly.

SUPPLIES

two to four players

small area with space for everyone to stand or sit

paper and pencil if you want to keep score

1 All players hide one of their hands behind their backs, holding up zero to five fingers on that hand.

2 At the count of three (or some other signal) all players bring their hands around and show how many fingers they're holding up.

3 The first player to correctly count and call out the total number of fingers wins a point. The sum must be correct to earn the point. If the sum is incorrect, no one gets a point and the next round begins.

4 You can keep playing until you reach 10 points or until you decide to stop.

The OLYMPICS and the THEATER

Ancient Greeks were a lot like people today. They liked to eat, have parties, and play music. They liked to talk about important issues. They also liked sports and going to the theater for a show. Because soldiers often had to fight hand-to-hand, sports were a way to train for war. After all, being a fast runner or good boxer came in handy on the battlefield!

Sports were also a way for Greeks to show off their fitness. (Remember, looking their best at all times was important to them.) Ancient Greeks were very competitive, and they held sports contests to see who was the best. Many city-states held regular contests during religious festivals. For example, Athens had an event called the Panathenaic Games. These games were held during the festival to honor Athena, the goddess of wisdom and protector of Athens. But, by far, the most popular contest was the Olympics.

THE ANCIENT OLYMPICS

The ancient Greeks held the Olympics until 393 CE. When the Romans took over Greece, they banned the Olympics. This is because the games worshipped ancient Greek gods and Rome was a Christian country. (Christianity is a one-god religion.) The Olympics could have been lost forever if it wasn't for the French baron Pierre de Coubertin. Inspired by the spirit of competition of the ancient games, he organized the first modern-day Olympics. They were held in Athens in 1896.

THE OLYMPICS

The ancient Greeks held the first Olympic games in 776 BCE. They were held in **Olympia**, a city-state in southern Greece, as part of a festival that honored the god Zeus. Like modern Olympics, the ancient games were held every four years. Men and boys came from all over Greece to compete. Foreigners and women were not allowed to compete. Greek women had their own games, though. They were called the Heraia.

Married women were not allowed to watch the games. This is because the athletes were naked! No one knows for certain why they didn't wear clothes while competing. One theory is that it was for safety. According to legend, an athlete's pants had once fallen down while he was running. He tripped, hit his head, and died. The more likely

JOKE TIME

Q: WHAT DID THE WINNER OF THE OLYMPIC RACE LOSE?

A: HIS BREATH!

explanation is that the ancient Greeks simply liked to show off just how fit they were. Plus, it was very hot. Going naked was probably more comfortable than wearing clothes. To enhance their physiques and to protect their skin from the drying sun, athletes covered themselves with olive oil.

People from as far away as Egypt came to admire the athletes' skill. The stadium in Olympia held over 40,000 spectators. And even more people came to sneak a peek or just be part of the five-day-long celebration. In fact, the Olympics were "the place to be." Greeks believed everyone should make the journey to see the games at least once in their life. Wars were even temporarily stopped so people could travel to the games. Although wars don't stop for the Olympic games today, countries often set aside their differences and try to get along while competing.

The ancient Olympic games were so popular, Olympia usually wasn't properly prepared for the crowds. They didn't have enough bedrooms, water, or even bathrooms for the guests. Spectators and athletes had to camp out and go to the bathroom outside, and they often fainted from dehydration.

THE SPORTS

Many of the ancient Olympic games are ones we're familiar with today. They included things like boxing, wrestling, horse and chariot racing, discus and javelin throwing, and long jumping.

WORDS to KNOW

OLYMPIA: a city-state in southern Greece where the ancient Olympic games took place.

PENTATHLON: an Olympic event that includes five sports. In ancient times, the contests included discus and javelin throwing, running, long jumping, and wrestling.

PANKRATION: a brutal sport of the ancient Greek Olympics that combined boxing and wrestling.

LAURELS: wreaths made of olive branches that Olympic winners wore on their heads.

ORCHESTRA: an area in front of the stage where the chorus performed in ancient Greek plays.

The games also included footraces. These sprints were the most popular sport.

The games also included a **pentathlon**, which means "five contests." The ancient Greek pentathlon included discus throwing, javelin throwing, running, long jumping, and wrestling. Today pentathlons include long-distance running, swimming, pistol shooting, fencing, and horseback riding.

Another popular event was **pankration**. It combined boxing and wrestling and was a little like what we call ultimate fighting. Fighters could do just about anything they wanted to their opponent. The only rule was no gouging the other person's eyes. As you can imagine, it was a dangerous sport. Many fighters died rather than give up.

Today, Olympians win gold, silver, and bronze medals. In ancient times, athletes won **laurels** made of olive tree leaves. Sometimes, they won a piece of pottery or the discus they threw. It may not sound like a lot, but there were other rewards for winning. Like many modern Olympians, ancient athletes enjoyed plenty of glory in their hometowns. They received gifts and free meals and were treated like heroes for the rest of their lives. No wonder so many athletes trained and made the long journey to the Olympics to compete!

COOL *artifact*

Ancient Greek long jumpers held stone weights in their hands. They swung the weights back and forth to get better forward momentum when they jumped.

THE THEATER

Going to the theater was another popular form of entertainment in ancient Greece. Like the Olympics, plays began as part of religious festivals. There were even contests (with prizes) to see who could write the best play. Soon, ancient Greeks began putting on plays all the time. Taxes and donations from wealthy citizens helped pay for the grand productions.

Plays took place in large theaters with tiers of stone seats. These theaters were built in a half–circle shape. This shape made the sound carry better. Theaters were often carved into the side of a hill or mountain. The seats faced the stage and there was a flat, round area called the **orchestra** in front of the stage. The orchestra was where the chorus performed. The chorus was

THEN & NOW

THEN: Ancient Greeks competed as individuals.

NOW: Many Olympic sports are team sports.

a group of dancers, musicians, and singers who helped explain the play to the audience. They were kind of like narrators. Outside the theater, vendors sold food, drinks, and cushions for the stone seats.

Only three actors stood on the stage at a time. Though women could go to the plays, they couldn't act in them. Men played all of the parts. The actors wore costumes. They also wore masks. These masks, made with stiff cloth, had exaggerated features so that the audience could see the mask more clearly. Some of the theaters could seat over 12,000 people, so people in the farthest seats had a hard time seeing small details.

The masks helped the audience tell who the character was and how he or she was feeling. For example, a mask might show that a character was an old woman who was sad. Many theater masks had two sides. This way, a character could change emotions quickly. All the actor had to do was flip the mask over. Scenery also helped the audience understand where the action took place.

Ancient Greeks performed many kinds of plays. But the most popular types of plays were comedies and tragedies. Comedies were usually about ordinary people in funny situations. Tragedies were sad plays. They were usually about Greek myths or gods and goddesses. Satires were also popular. These were plays that poked fun at leaders or serious issues.

MAKE A
Laurel Wreath

SUPPLIES

6 green pipe cleaners

scissors

1 or 2 packages of silk leaves with wire stems, from a craft store

1 First you'll make a headband out of pipe cleaners. Twist two pipe cleaners together to make one strong piece. Do this a total of three times. Then twist the ends of the three lengths of pipe cleaner together to make one long piece.

2 Wrap the pipe cleaner around your head. The band should be snug. Be sure you can put it on and take it off easily.

3 Once you have the right size circle, tie off the ends and trim off any extra. Or you can twist any extra length around the rest of the pipe cleaners.

4 Attach the leaves to the headband by wrapping the stem wires around the pipe cleaner headband. Make sure all the leaves are going in the same direction.

5 Keep adding leaves until you've gone all around the handband. Add as many leaves as you'd like.

6 Now that you're done, why not put on your own Olympic games with some friends? You can make laurel wreaths for everyone!

MAKE LONG JUMP
HandWeights

Some of the hand weights that ancient Olympic long jumpers used were simple stones. Some were fancy enough to have grooves for the athletes fingers. Here's an easy way to make a pair of hand weights, or halteres. You'll be using spray paint, so ask an adult for help.

1 Fill the orange juice cans with sand or rice, as full as possible. Place the lids on the cans. Secure them tightly with a long piece of duct tape.

SUPPLIES

2 small orange juice cans with lids, cleaned and dried

sand OR rice, or dried beans

duct tape

newspaper

gray spray paint

2 Spread your work space with newspaper. Follow the directions on the can to spray paint the cans and lids. You'll have to spray paint in two steps so you can get the bottom of the cans, too.

3 When the paint is dry, try out the weights. Hold one in each hand and stand with your feet about shoulders' width apart. Bend your legs slightly and swing your arms (and the weights) back and forth together a few times. Pull your arms back and then jump as you bring them forward. The weights should help move you forward. Try doing a long jump both with the weights and without the weights. Do the weights help you jump farther?

MAKE A Theater Mask

SUPPLIES

- heavy cardboard
- pointy scissors
- pencil
- glue or tape
- thick craft stick or tongue depressor
- craft paint and markers, various colors
- yarn

1 Ask an adult to help you with the scissors. Cut the cardboard into a large circle. An easy way to do this is to lay a dinner plate on top of the cardboard and trace the plate.

2 Hold the cardboard up to your face. Ask a friend to help you make two pencil marks where your eyes are.

3 Pull the mask away from your face and carefully cut two holes for your eyes with the pointy scissors.

4 Spread glue on half of the craft stick and attach it to the bottom of your mask. This will be your mask's handle. You can use tape if you don't want to wait for the glue to dry.

5 Use the paint and markers to decorate each side of the mask. You could make the same character with different expressions. Or you could create two entirely different characters.

6 Glue pieces of the yarn on your mask to create hair. When your mask is done, you can put on your own play! Use the handle to turn your mask from one side to the other.

DEMOCRACY and WAR

Early in the history of ancient Greece kings ruled city-states. Later on, a small group of wealthy people ruled. But in Athens, something special happened around 500 BCE. People came up with a new way to run things. This form of government is called **democracy**. In a democracy, people have a say in how their government runs things. The word *democracy* means "people's rule."

WORDS to KNOW

DEMOCRACY: a form of government where the people have a say in decisions.

ASSEMBLY: a group of 6,000 citizens in ancient Greece who met, discussed, and then voted on important matters in Athens.

COUNCIL: a group of 500 ancient Greeks who made laws and chose military leaders.

JUROR: someone who is part of a jury.

JURY: a group of people who hear a case in court. Jurors give their opinion, called a verdict.

TALLY: count.

The main feature of Athens' democracy was the **Assembly**. It was a kind of like a town meeting. Any citizen could be a part of the Assembly. But only free men who were born in Athens were citizens. Women, slaves, and foreigners were not citizens. In the Assembly, citizens voiced their opinions and voted on big decisions, such as whether or not to go to war. The people in the Assembly voted by raising their hands. The majority won.

Assembly took place every ten days. In order for the Assembly to be official, 6,000 people needed to show up. If there were not enough people, a special patrol went looking for more. Anyone they found trying to get out of their duty got their tunic marked with red paint. They also had to pay a fine.

There was a smaller group of people within the Assembly that was called the **Council**. They handled day-to-day things like making laws

VOTING OUT LEADERS

If the people of Athens didn't like a leader, they had a way to get rid of him. They just took a vote. Everyone gathered and wrote on a piece of broken pottery the name of the leader they wanted out. If the person received more than 600 votes, he was kicked out of Athens for ten years.

THEN & NOW

THEN: The people of Athens were the first to try democracy.

NOW: Greece is a republic, and the people still have a say in how things are run.

and creating policies. This group had 500 members. They took turns meeting. Fifty members at a time met at a round building called the Tholos. Council members were chosen from the Assembly and served on the Council for one year. The Council voted to choose the people who led the military. They were called *strategoi*.

JUSTICE

Ancient Greek citizens had to be a part of the Assembly. They also had to serve as **jurors** every once in a while. Ancient Greeks thought sitting on a **jury** was kind of exciting. Jurors had to be at least 30 years old and citizens of Athens. They were picked at random. Juries were usually pretty large, with 200 to 500 members. The large number made it harder for the accused to pay members to vote in his favor. It also made it harder for there to be a tie. Today, most juries have 12 members.

Unlike today, there were no judges. There weren't any lawyers either. The person accused of a crime made a speech to tell his side of the story. He was all alone! (If he wanted, he could have someone else write the speech, though.) When he was done, the jury voted. To vote, jurors used small bronze tokens.

AND THAT'S WHY I'M INNOCENT!

A "guilty" token had a hole in the middle of it. An "innocent" token had no hole. All of the tokens went into a clay jar. Then they were **tallied**. Sentencing happened right after the tally.

In Athens, punishment didn't usually mean jail. Some guilty people had to pay a fine. Others lost their rights or some of their possessions. Jail was saved for serious things like murder. (Jurors jailed Socrates, the famous philosopher, for corrupting the youth of Athens.) After spending some time in jail, prisoners were put to death in cruel ways. For example, they were beheaded, stoned to death, or poisoned.

SOLDIERS

Ancient Greece had many city-states. And the city-states didn't always get along. Actually, they fought a lot! To protect themselves, the people of Athens built a strong army. This army had soldiers who rode horses, called **cavalry**. Other groups, called auxiliaries, included stone throwers and archers. But the backbone of Athens' army was its foot soldiers.

Greek foot soldiers were called **hoplites**. A hoplite started training at age 18. He trained for two years. Hoplites were not paid. They even had to provide their own weapons and armor. The word *hoplite* comes from the word *hoplon*, which means "shield." But a big, round shield made of **bronze** or leather wasn't the only type of armor a hoplite used. Hoplites also wore helmets. These helmets often had crests made of animal hair. Some had a plate to cover the soldier's nose or long sides to cover his cheeks. Other helmets had holes for a soldier's mouth or ears.

Hoplites used bronze breastplates to protect their torsos. These breastplates were made especially for the wearer. They had two sides. One covered the front of the body and one covered the back. Leather straps connected them. The fronts of a soldier's legs, from the knee to the ankle, were protected by greaves. Greaves looked a lot like the shin guards a soccer player wears. Greaves were also made of bronze.

Hoplites sometimes carried short swords into battle. But a Greek soldier's main weapon was a long spear. Soldiers used their shields and spears in a formation called a phalanx. To make a **phalanx**, soldiers lined up close together, with their shields up, to form a block. The block of soldiers could then push itself through groups of enemy soldiers. The ancient Greek army used other tactics, too. A common plan of attack was to simply surround the enemy's city. Eventually the city ran out of food and surrendered. This was called a siege. Ancient Greeks also used moveable towers and battering rams to gain access to a city.

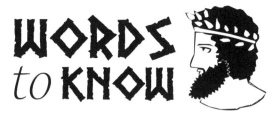

WORDS to KNOW

CAVALRY: soldiers on horses.

HOPLITE: a Greek foot soldier.

BRONZE: a hard metal made of a mixture of copper and another metal, such as tin.

PHALANX: a group of soliders standing close together.

ALLIANCE: a group of people who join together and agree to help each other if one member is attacked.

ALEXANDER THE GREAT

One of ancient Greece's best military leaders was Alexander the Great. Alexander was the son of a powerful king named Phillip II of Macedonia.

When he was a young boy, the famous philosopher Aristotle tutored him. Alexander took over for his dad when he was just twenty years old. Over the next eleven years, Alexander led his large and powerful army over thousands of miles. Along the way, Alexander invaded many lands, including the Persian Empire. This included places we call the Middle East, Turkey, Egypt, and Afghanistan. Basically, Alexander conquered the entire world that was known in ancient times!

It is said that Alexander the Great never lost a battle. But conquering new lands and greatly expanding the Greek empire wasn't the only thing Alexander was good at. He was very good at treating the people he conquered kindly. And he worked together to blend cultures. For instance, he encouraged his soldiers to marry women from the newly conquered lands. His actions helped to bring about a period of history that was peaceful for ancient Greece. Alexander died at age 33 of a fever.

☐ ALEXANDER THE GREAT'S EMPIRE

COOL *artifact*

Alexander the Great even established a few cities. For example, the great city of Alexandria, Egypt, was named after him. And the ancient city of Bucephala was named after Alexander's horse, Bucephalus.

COOL *artifact*

When the Athenians won the Battle of Marathon, the army's leader sent a messenger back to Athens. According to the legend, the messenger ran the 25 miles from Marathon to Athens without stopping. When he got there, he announced the news and then fell down dead from exhaustion. This is how today's marathon race was born.

TWO IMPORTANT WARS

Ancient Greeks fought many wars. Among the most important ones were the Persian Wars and the Peloponnesian War.

Persia was a land in the country that is now called Iran. In the 500s BCE, the Persians began taking over the city-states that were located in modern-day Turkey. The Persian king put a man named Aristagoras in charge. Aristagoras didn't agree with the way the king wanted him to rule, so he led a rebellion. He went to Athens for help. The Athenians agreed to help and took part in burning Sardis, an important city. Of course the Persians weren't happy about this. They decided Athens should be punished. This was the start of the Persian Wars.

First, the Persians attacked Athens at Marathon, a nearby city. The Athenian army was outnumbered.

JOKE TIME

Q: WHAT DO YOU CALL THE MILITARY LEADER WHO MISSED THE BATTLE BECAUSE HE OVERSLEPT?

A: ALEXANDER THE LATE!

But using their phalanx formation, they defeated the Persians. It was a great victory, but that wasn't the end of things. The Persians attacked several times over the next years. One of the last attacks came by sea. With only 300 ships, the Greek army managed to hold off 800 Persian ships. They did this by cleverly luring the Persian ships into a strait. This is a narrow stretch of water between two bodies of land. Since the Persian ships couldn't move or turn around, it was easy for the Greeks to sink them. After this defeat, the Persians finally decided to give up and go home.

After the Persian Wars, Athens decided to form an **alliance** with other city-states. This way, they could join soldiers, weapons, and money and be ready if there was another war. Not everybody wanted to join, though. Sparta was a rival of Athens. It was one of the city-states that didn't want to join the alliance. One reason was that Athens was taking all the money the alliance was saving for war. Eventually the two city-states began to argue. Soon, war broke out between Athens and Sparta. This war is known as the Peloponnesian War.

Athens and Sparta continued to fight for many years. Sparta destroyed Athens' fleet of ships. Without ships, the people of Athens couldn't get food they needed from other countries. So Sparta won the war. But even though they won, the war took a lot out of Sparta. It took a lot out of Athens, too. Unfortunately, neither city-state was ever as strong as it had been before the war.

ATHENS IS THE BEST!

SPARTA IS THE BEST!

MAKE
Jury Tokens

SUPPLIES

½ cup fine sawdust from a hardware store with bits of wood or splinters removed

¼ cup flour

bowl

water

wax paper

butter knife

bronze acrylic paint

1 Use your hands to combine the sawdust and flour in the bowl. Slowly add a little water. Knead the dough until it is stiff. Though it will be stiff, you should still be able to mold it with your hands. Keep kneading until the dough has a stretchy feel to it.

2 Dump the dough onto a piece of wax paper. Roll and pat the dough into a disc that is about the size of a half-dollar and about a quarter-inch thick. You can use the knife to cut the dough if you'd like. This will be your *not guilty* token.

3 Make another disc. Use the knife to carefully cut a hole in the center of this token. This will be your *guilty* token. Let the tokens dry completely. When they're done, you can paint them. Now, you're ready to vote like an ancient Greek!

MAKE A Water

Ancient Greeks kept track of time during trials and government proceedings by using a water clock. Their water clocks used simple clay pots. Here is an easy way to make your own water clock using modern materials. You'll be using sharp scissors, so ask an adult for help.

SUPPLIES

2 plastic containers, one smaller than the other one

ruler

duct tape

pointy scissors

measuring cup

water

stopwatch

1 Set the larger of the two containers on a flat surface. Tape the ruler up the back side of the container. The ruler should be vertical.

2 Use the pointy scissors to poke a very small hole in the middle of the bottom of the smaller container. The hole should allow water to drip out steadily, but not pour out. To test this, add some water to the container and hold it over a sink. If the water drips out too slowly, make the hole a little bit bigger. If the water pours out, you can make the hole smaller by putting a piece of duct tape over part of the hole.

Clock

3 After you get the drip hole just right, tape the small container to the top of the ruler. The small container should be directly above the larger container.

4 Pour ¼ cup of water into the top container. Start the stopwatch. See how long it takes for all of the water to drip into the larger container.

5 How long did it take? Try experimenting with more or less water to see if you can get your water clock to keep time for 1 minute, then 2 minutes, then 5 minutes.

MAKE A Pair of

You'll be using a hammer and a nail and spray paint for this project. Ask an adult for help.

SUPPLIES

- a partner to help
- newspaper
- plastic wrap
- plaster cloth, sometimes called plaster gauze, cut into medium-size pieces (Rigid Wrap is one brand found at craft stores)
- bowl of water
- hammer
- nail
- bronze spray paint
- 4 pairs leather shoe laces

1 Spread newspaper on the floor. Sit down with your legs straight out in front of you. Cover your lower legs with plastic wrap.

2 Dip pieces of plaster cloth into the water. Lay the wet pieces on top of your shins. Keep adding pieces until you have several layers. Have your partner help with this step.

3 Sit still while the plaster cloth begins to dry and set. This should take about 10 to 15 minutes. Carefully pull the plaster and plastic off your legs. It won't be completely dry, but it should hold its shape.

Greaves

4 Lay the plaster greaves to dry on the newspaper. Switch places with your partner so he or she can make a pair of greaves, too!

5 Once the plaster is dry (this will take several days), peel off the plastic wrap. Use the hammer and nail to poke four holes in each plaster greave. Two holes should be close to the top, one on each side. The other two holes should be close to the bottom, one on each side.

6 Follow the directions on the spray can to paint the fronts and backs of the greaves. Let the paint dry. Finally, thread a shoe lace through each hole. Make a knot at the end so that they can't slip out. Use the laces to tie the guards to your legs.

MAKE A
Hoplite Shield

1 Cut the cardboard into a circle with a diameter of between 12 and 18 inches. You can make your shield whatever size would work best for you.

2 Use the markers or paint to create your own shield design. The ancient Greeks got to design their own shields, too!

3 When your design is finished, turn the cardboard over. Make sure the top of your design is still at the top when you flip the cardboard. Glue the ends of one piece of foam to the back left side of the cardboard to form a strap. Important: don't lay the foam flat. You need to be able to slide your arm in behind it.

SUPPLIES

large piece of thick cardboard

ruler

scissors

markers or paint

2 pieces of brown craft foam, 11 inches by 2 inches

glue

4 Glue the ends of the second piece of foam to the back right side of the cardboard to form a second handle. When the glue is dry, you're ready to fend off an enemy attack! To use your shield, just slip one arm through both straps and hold the shield in front of you!

GODS, GODDESSES
and MYTHS

Ancient Greeks didn't have churches. They didn't have holy books or religious leaders. You might think that religion wasn't important to them. But it was! Religion was part of their everyday lives. Ancient Greeks just didn't believe in one god. They believed in many gods. There were twelve main gods, though. They were sometimes called the Olympian gods. This is because they supposedly lived on **Mount Olympus**, the highest mountain in Greece.

These gods and goddesses were thought to be a lot like people. The ancient Greeks believed the gods fell in love, married, had kids, got angry and jealous, and enjoyed music and dancing. The ancient Greeks also believed the gods were involved with people's everyday lives. They believed that gods controlled things like the weather and illnesses. Each god or goddess had a special thing to take care of.

Ancient Greeks worshipped gods and goddesses at festivals throughout the year. They also worshipped at home each day. Every family had an **altar** in their courtyard, where they left offerings for the gods. These offerings could be food, or gold and silver. When they were ill or hurt and wanted a god to help them, ancient Greeks left

OLYMPIAN GODS

Zeus: the king of all the gods. Zeus was in charge of earth and heaven

Hera: Zeus's wife and the goddess of women and marriage.

Apollo: god of music and fortune-telling and Artemis's twin.

Artemis: goddess of nature and Apollo's twin.

Athena: goddess of wisdom

Ares: god of war.

Aphrodite: goddess of love and beauty.

Demeter: goddess of grain and the harvest.

Hades: god of the underworld

Hermes: the messenger of the gods. He was also in charge of taking the dead to the underworld.

Hephaestus: god of fire.

Poseidon: god of the sea.

votives. Votives were models of the body part that needed healing. Public prayers were also a part of all government proceedings.

Though they didn't have official religious leaders, the ancient Greeks did have **oracles**. Oracles were women who supposedly spoke for the gods. Ancient Greeks came to them for advice about all kinds of things. Sometimes, their advice was good. But most of their advice was too vague to be helpful.

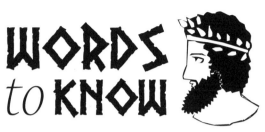

WORDS to KNOW

MOUNT OLYMPUS: where the ancient Greek gods lived.

ALTAR: a raised table for religous ceremonies.

VOTIVE: something that is a symbol for a wish.

ORACLES: women who supposedly spoke for the gods and offered advice.

MYTHS

Myths are stories that teach a lesson or explain how something in the world came to be. The gods and goddesses showed up a lot in Greek myths. There are hundreds of Greeks myths. Some are about the constellations of stars. Others are about legendary soldiers who won battles against great odds. Many Greek myths are very familiar. For example, maybe you've heard about Midas, Medusa, and Achilles.

Midas was a peasant who the gods made into a king. King Midas wanted to be the richest king in the world. He thought nothing in the world was more important than money. And when the god Dionysus granted him a wish, King Midas jumped at the chance. He wished that everything he touched would turn to gold.

At first, Midas loved his gift. But soon, he discovered he couldn't eat or drink because these things turned to gold, too. And when Midas accidentally turned his daughter into gold, he was terribly sad. He begged and begged Dionysus to undo the wish. Dionysus finally agreed.

He told King Midas to bathe in the Pactolus River. According to the myth, this is why that river's bank had lots of gold in ancient times.

Medusa was a girl who the god Poseidon liked. He flirted with her at Athena's temple. Athena thought this was disrespectful, so she turned Medusa into a creature with snakes in place of hair. If that wasn't bad enough, the curse caused anyone who looked at Medusa's head to turn to stone! A man named Perseus set off to kill Medusa. Athena helped him by holding up a shield. By seeing Medusa in the shield's reflection (instead of looking directly at her), Perseus was able to kill Medusa. This story is a lesson about the rewards of cleverness.

Achilles was the son of a fairy. According to a fortune-teller, Achilles was destined to be a great soldier. Achilles's mom wasn't happy about this. Like all moms, she worried about her son's safety. To protect her baby, she dipped him in the River Styx. This was supposed to make him impossible to kill. The problem was that Achilles's heel didn't get dipped in the water. Achilles grew up and did become a great soldier. Sadly, during a battle in the Trojan War, someone shot a poisoned arrow into Achilles's heel and he died. The lesson of the story of Achilles is that everyone has a weakness.

THEN & NOW

THEN: Ancient Greeks had no official religion.

NOW: The official religion of Greece is Eastern Orthodox Christianity.

UNDERWORLD FERRY

Ancient Greeks believed that when people died, they went to the River Styx, the river between Earth and the **underworld**. There, a god ferried them across the river to be judged. Since the ferry captain had to be paid, families put a coin inside a dead person's pocket.

THE TROJAN WAR

Another place where the gods and goddesses show up frequently is in stories of the Trojan War. The Trojan War is one of the most famous wars of all time. The only thing is, we don't know for certain whether it really took place! The storyteller Homer tells us about the war in his long poem, *The Iliad*. The city of Troy (where the war took place) might have been real. Then again, it might not have been. In the late 1800s, a German archeologist named Heinrich Schliemann found what might be Troy's remains in Turkey. Some people believe the Trojan War might have been several, real wars whose tales got mixed together. But whether it was real or not, the Trojan War is a great story.

According to Homer, the war started when some goddesses argued about who was the most beautiful. Zeus sent a man named Paris (a Trojan) to settle the argument. Paris picked the goddess Aphrodite.

JOKE TIME

Q: WHAT WOULD BE A GOOD NICKNAME FOR THE GREEK SOLDIERS WHO HID INSIDE THE TROJAN HORSE?

A: THE HORSE FORCE!

As a reward, Aphrodite promised Paris he could marry any woman he wanted. Paris wanted Helen, said to be the most beautiful woman in the world. The only problem was that Helen was already married to a Greek man! Her husband wasn't happy when Helen and Paris ran away together. (Some versions of the story say Helen was kidnapped.) He and his allies banded together to get her back.

For ten years, the Trojans and Greeks battled, and different gods and goddesses took sides and intervened. For example, Apollo sent a plague to the Greek camp. A plague is a terrible, contagious disease.

In the end, the Greeks defeated the Trojans in a very sneaky way. First they built a large wooden horse. Then they pretended to surrender and left the horse as a gift outside the walls of Troy. The Trojans, not knowing

THERE'S HELEN. SHE'S SO BEAUTIFUL!

YES! SHE SMILED AT ME! SHE REALLY DID!

that Greek soldiers were hiding inside the horse, brought it inside the city. That night, while the Trojans slept, the Greek soldiers snuck out of the horse. The Trojans were caught by surprise and had no choice but to surrender. This is where we get the phrase "beware of Greeks bearing gifts." It means "don't trust your enemies."

TEMPLES

Ancient Greeks are famous for their beautiful temples. These buildings weren't churches. People didn't meet at them to worship together or listen to someone preach. Ancient Greek temples were the gods' and goddesses' homes. And since they belonged to the gods, the ancient Greeks built them with great care and in grand style. Temples were often made out of marble or limestone and had fancy tile roofs. Many of them had columns and large statues of the gods. Beautiful bands of carved scenes, called **friezes**, decorated the outsides of temples.

The most famous and grandest of all ancient Greek temples is the Parthenon. It was dedicated to the goddesses Athena and built on Athens' acropolis. Like most temples, it was a rectangular building with a triangular roof. It was much bigger than most temples, though.

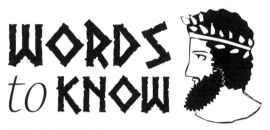

UNDERWORLD: in mythology, the place beneath the earth where it was believed the souls of the dead go.

FRIEZE: a band of carved artwork around the outside of a building that usually tells a story or shows a scene.

Many temples served as storage areas for valuables. Ancient Greeks believed no one would rob a god!

GREEK COLUMNS

The columns of the Parthenon are called Doric columns. They have thick bottoms and plain tops. This was a very common column style in ancient Greece. Ionic columns were also common. These were a bit thinner and had fancy, scroll-like tops. Corinthian columns were a little less common. These columns had elaborate, leafy tops.

It was nearly 240 feet long, 110 feet wide, and 60 feet tall. It had 8 columns on each end and 17 columns along each side.

The Parthenon was made of marble and had wooden beams that supported the marble ceiling. A splendid 45-foot-tall statue of Athena stood inside. The sculptor carved this statue out of ivory. Precious jewels were used for the eyes. And the clothes were made out of thin pieces of gold. It took 15 years to build the Parthenon. In its day, it stood as a great symbol of Athens' beauty and power. Throughout history, fire that burned wooden beams, war, and invasions took their toll on the magnificent building. Fortunately, part of it still remains for us to see today.

PLAY MEDUSA FREEZE TAG

According to the myth, Athena cursed Medusa, who become a creature who could turn people into stone. In this game, we pretend that Athena feels bad about what she did and helps Medusa's victims.

SUPPLIES

a bunch of friends

a large area to run around in

1 Choose one player to be Medusa. This person will be the tagger. Choose another player to be Athena. This person will help the people who have been tagged.

2 Everyone gathers in a group. This includes Medusa and Athena. On the count of three, everyone scatters.

3 Medusa's job is to turn players into stone. She (or he) does this by tagging someone. Once a person is tagged, he or she must stay perfectly still.

4 Athena can free a stone person by tagging him or her. After a while, Medusa and Athena can choose other players to take their places.

MAKE A Trojan

1 Cut four circles out of the cardboard. They should be about the size of half-dollars. Lay the shoebox lid down so that the top of it is facing up. Glue the cardboard "wheels" to the sides of the lid. It doesn't matter that the wheels don't really spin. They are just for decoration. This is the base for your horse. Set it aside for now.

2 Lay the shoebox on top of the cardboard. Trace around the box. Cut along the pencil lines to make a cardboard rectangle. Place this piece of cardboard on top of the open shoebox. Tape one long side of the cardboard to the shoebox to make a flap lid on the shoebox.

3 Glue or tape the four toilet paper rolls to the bottom of the shoebox. These will be your horse's legs.

4 Glue or tape the plastic cup to one end of the shoebox. This will be your horse's head. Now, glue the entire horse (feet down) on top of the base.

5 Tear the masking tape into long strips. Cover your horse and the base horizontally with the strips. The strips of tape will help make your horse look like it's made of pieces of wood.

6 Once the horse and base are covered in tape, paint everything brown. Be sure to cover your work space in newspaper first!

Horse

7 When the paint is dry, use the craft foam to make a mane, ears, and a tail for your horse. Attach it with tape.

8 Now, you can hide money, jewelry, or other secret stuff in your Trojan horse!

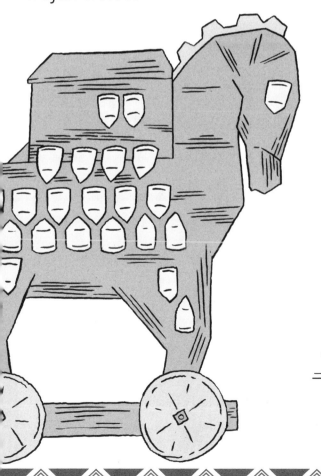

SUPPLIES

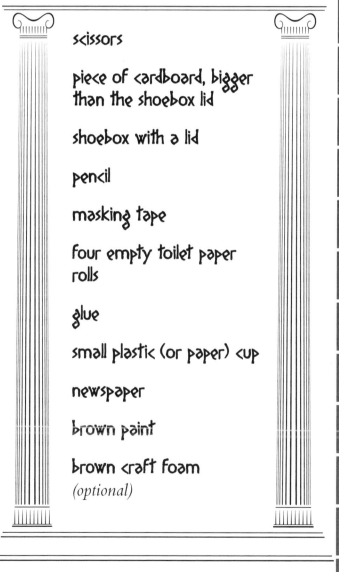

scissors

piece of cardboard, bigger than the shoebox lid

shoebox with a lid

pencil

masking tape

four empty toilet paper rolls

glue

small plastic (or paper) cup

newspaper

brown paint

brown craft foam
(optional)

MAKE A
Midas Meal

You'll be using spray paint so be sure to have an adult handy.

1 Cover your work space with newspaper. Glue the paper plate, paper cup, fork, spoon, and knife to the placemat.

2 Use the air-hardening clay to create food for your plate. For example, you could make olives, grapes, fish, and a roll. Get creative, and have fun thinking up a good meal. What kind of food would you like to eat? When you're done, let the clay harden.

3 Once the clay food is hard, glue it onto your plate. Follow the directions on the can to spray paint the placemat and everything on it. When the paint is dry, you'll have a place setting fit for a king—King Midas, that is!

SUPPLIES

newspaper

paper plate

paper or plastic cup

plastic fork, spoon, and knife

glue

inexpensive plastic placemat

air-hardening clay

gold spray paint

ABACUS: a counting tool made with beads strung on wires that the ancient Greeks used to solve math problems.

ACROPOLIS: an area of high ground, such as a steep hill, where people gathered for safety during a battle. When people talk about "the Acropolis," they mean the one in Athens.

AGORA: the open marketplace in the middle of an ancient Greek town.

ALLIANCE: a group of people who join together and agree to help each other if one member is attacked.

ALTAR: a raised table for religious ceremonies.

AMPHORAE: rounded clay containers with long necks that the ancient Greeks put olive oil and wine in.

ANDRON: the area of a Greek home where the men would entertain guests and hold dinner parties.

ANDRONITIS: the men's area of an ancient Greek home.

ASSEMBLY: a group of 6,000 ancient Greeks who met, discussed, and then voted on important matters in Athens.

ATHENS: the biggest and most powerful polis in ancient Greece.

BOW: the front of a boat.

BRONZE: a hard metal made of a mixture of copper and another metal, such as tin.

BROOCH: a special pin.

CAVALRY: soldiers on horseback.

CHITON: a piece of clothing that men and women wore in ancient Greek times.

CIRCUMFERENCE: the distance around a circle.

CHLAMYS: a short cloak worn by ancient Greeks.

CITY-STATE: an independent village or town in ancient Greece.

COMEDY: a play about ordinary people in funny situations.

COURTYARD: the small open-roofed area in the center of an ancient Greek home.

DEBATE: to argue about something, trying to convince the other person of a point of view.

DEMOCRACY: a form of government where the people participate.

DIAMETER: the distance across a circle through the middle.

DIONYSOS: the god of wine.

FERMENT: when a substance breaks down over time into another substance, such as grape juice turning into wine.

FRIEZE: a band of carved artwork around the outside of a building that usually tells a story or shows a scene.

GYNAECONITIS: the women's area of an ancient Greek home.

HIMATION: a large piece of material that the ancient Greeks wore over their shoulders.

HOMER: a famous ancient Greek poet who wrote *The Iliad* and *The Odyssey*.

HOPLITE: a Greek foot soldier.

JUROR: someone who is part of a jury.

JURY: a group of people, called jurors, who hear a case in court. Jurors give their opinion, called a verdict

KLINES: long couches that were used at ancient Greek dinner parties. Guests ate lying down.

KYLIX: a shallow, two-handled cup use for drinking wine.

LAURELS: wreaths made of olive branches that Olympic winners in ancient Greece wore on their heads.

LONG WALLS: long stone walls that protected the road between Athens and the port of Piraeus.

MERCHANT SHIP: cargo ships important for trade.

MOUNT OLYMPUS: where the ancient Greek gods lived.

OIKOS: everyone who was part of an ancient Greek household.

OLYMPIA: a city-state in southern Greece where the ancient Olympic games took place.

ORCHESTRA: an area in front of the stage where the chorus performed in ancient Greek plays.

ORACLES: women who supposedly spoke for the gods and offered advice.

PANKRATION: a brutal sport of the ancient Greek Olympics that combined boxing and wrestling.

PAPYRUS: paper made from pressing a reed plant that is also called papyrus.

PENTATHLON: an Olympic event that includes five sports. In ancient times, the contests included discus and javelin throwing, running, long jumping and wrestling.

PETASOS: a flat, wide-brimmed hat that ancient Greeks wore.

PHALANX: a group of soldiers standing close together.

PHILOSOPHY: the love of and search for wisdom.

PI: The number represented by the symbol π and often shortened to 3.14.

PLAINS: large, flat, land areas.

POLEIS: Greek city-states. Just one is called a polis.

SATIRE: plays that poke fun at leaders or serious issues.

SIEGE: surrounding a place and cutting it off from supplies.

SYMPOSIUM: a party at which ancient Greek men would drink, sing, and discuss politics and philosophy.

TALLY: count.

THALAMOS: the master bedroom of an ancient Greek home.

TRAGEDY: a sad play, usually about gods and goddesses and Greek myths in ancient Greece.

TRIREME: a Greek warship powered by a large crew of oarsmen.

UNDERWORLD: in mythology, the place beneath the earth where it was believed the souls of the dead go.

VOTIVE: something that is a symbol for a wish.

Adkins, Lesley, and Roy Adkins. *Handbook to Life in Ancient Greece.* New York, NY: Facts on File, 2005.

Bordessa, Kris. *Tools of the Ancient Greeks.* White River Junction, VT: Nomad Press, 2006.

Chisholm, Jane, Lisa Miles, and Struan Reid. *The Usborne Internet-Linked Encyclopedia of Ancient Greece.* London, England: Usborne Publishing Ltd., 2002.

Connolly, Peter. *Ancient Greece.* Oxford, England: Oxford University Press, 2001.

Connolly, Peter, and Hazel Dodge. *The Ancient City: Life in Classical Athens and Rome.* Oxford, England: Oxford University Press, 1998.

Curlee, Lynn. *Parthenon.* New York, NY: Atheneum Books for Young Children, 2004.

Dersin, Denise, ed. *What Life Was Like at the Dawn of Democracy: Classical Athens 525–322 BC.* New York, NY: Time-Life Books, 1997.

Edmondson, Elizabeth. *The Trojan War.* London, England: Hodder Children's Books, 1992.

Hicks, Peter. *History Beneath Your Feet: Ancient Greece.* Austin, TX: Steck-Vaughn Publishing, 2000.

Nardo, Don. *Life in Ancient Greece.* San Diego, CA: Lucent Books, 1996.

Pearson, Anne. *Ancient Greece.* New York, NY. DK Publishing,1992.

Perrottet, Tony. *The Naked Olympics.* New York, NY: Random House Publishing Group, 2004.

Pipe, Jim. *Mystery History of the Trojan Horse.* London, England: Aladdin Books Ltd., 1997.

Tames, Richard. *Ancient Greek Children.* Chicago, IL: Heinemann Library, 2003.

WANT TO READ MORE? TRY THESE BOOKS!

The Crafts and Cultures of the Ancient Greeks by Joann Jovinelly and Jason Netelkos from The Rosen Publishing Group, Inc. 2002.

Adventures in Ancient Greece by Linda Bailey from Kids Can Press, 2005.

Ancient Greece: Modern Rhymes for Ancient Times by Susan Altman from Children's Press, 2001.

You Wouldn't Want to Be a Slave in Ancient Greece! by Fiona MacDonald, David Salariya, and David Antram from Franklin Watts, 2000.

If I Were a Kid in Ancient Greece from Cobblestone Publishing, 2007.

Ancient Greece and the Olympics by Mary Pope Osborne and Natalie Pope Boyce from Random House for Young Readers, 2004.

I Wonder Why Greeks Built Temples and Other Questions About Ancient Greece by Fiona MacDonald from Kingfisher, 2006.

COOL MUSEUMS TO VISIT

The Cleveland Museum of Art (Cleveland, Ohio)

The Metropolitan Museum of Art (New York, New York)

Los Angeles County Museum of Art (Los Angeles, California)

The Detroit Institute of Arts (Detroit, Michigan)

Museum of Fine Arts (Boston, Massachusetts)

Nelson-Atkins Museum of Art (Kansas City, Missouri)

University of Pennsylvania Museum of Archaeology and Anthropology (Philadelphia, Pennsylvania)

COOL WEBSITES TO CHECK OUT

A to Z Kidstuff
http://www.atozkidsstuff.com/greece.html

Ancient Greece
http://www.ancientgreece.com/s/Main_Page/

British Museum—Ancient Greece
http://www.ancientgreece.co.uk/

Suffolk Web: Ancient Histories
http://www.suffolk.lib.ny.us/youth/jcancient.html

Cyber Sleuth Kids: Ancient Civilizations
http://cybersleuth-kids.com/sleuth/History/Ancient_Civilizations/Greece/index.htm

History for Kids—Ancient Greece
http://www.historyforkids.org/learn/greeks/

Mr. Donn Organization
http://greece.mrdonn.org/